How to Make Tiny
Paper Mache Dogs

With Patterns
for 27 Different Breeds

By Jonni Good

Wet Cat Books, Brookings, South Dakota

Published by Wet Cat Books
909 3rd Street
Brookings, SD 57006
http://WetCatBooks.com

Good, Jonni
How to Make Tiny Paper Mache Dogs: With Patterns
for 27 Different Breeds

ISBN: 978-0-9741065-5-7

Contents

IntroDuction

In this book you'll discover how easy and fun it can be to create an interesting little sculpture of your favorite canine friend.

I want you to enjoy sculpting as much as I Do...

And what could be more enjoyable than putting the finishing touches on a little sculpture that came out exactly the way you wanted it to? That's the "magic" of using patterns for your sculptures.

These little dogs cost almost nothing to make and they go together fast, but you'll be using the same artistic methods used by professional sculptors:

1. Create a simple wire armature based on the bones of your favorite breed. (The patterns in the book make it easy.)

2. Add foil and tape to the wire armature. At first you'll work on getting the silhouette right, because that's the key to creating a successful sculpture. (The patterns make that easy, too.)

3. Then fill in the rest of the body with more foil and tape. (The sculptures are too small to worry about tiny details.)

4. Now it's time to bend the leg joints, spine and tail into a posture that captures the individual personality of your dog.

5. Then add two layers of newspaper and paste.

6. And Paint.

When you're finished, you'll have a unique sculpture that you designed all by yourself, and I guarantee you'll have fun doing it!

Why Dogs?

Well, because we love them, of course. Plus, their familiar behaviors and postures make them ideal subjects for dynamic little sculptures based on a wire armature. Since dogs communicate through body language, you give your sculpted dog a specific mood or attitude just by bending the wire armatures at the joints.

Your little pooch might beg for a tummy rub. Or maybe it wants a game of tag like the terrier on the cover. Or maybe it's waiting patiently for its favorite human to come home from school, or it's taking a nap, or begging for a treat. It's totally up to you.

Since your sculpted dog can do anything that *real* dogs can do, the possible variations for unique sculptures are almost limitless. It's the wire armatures that make that possible.

Why Paper Mache?

If you've visited my blog or read one of my previous books, you know that my house if full of sculptures and masks. Most of them depict animals of one kind or another, and almost all of them are made with some form of paper mache. I love this stuff!

Paper mache is cheap, and you don't have to go to art school to figure out how to use it. You can get paper mache materials almost anywhere—in fact, most of the supplies used in this book are probably already lying around your house.

Some people look down on paper mache *because* it's affordable, but that's just silly. When you build with paper and paste you're following a long, venerable tradition. Paper mache was first invented in China as a way to use up every last scrap of precious paper, back when each sheet was hand-made by skilled craftsmen. (They made military helmets out of it). Now, several thousand years later, paper is machine-made, cheap and abundant, and our garbage dumps are full of it—but it's *still* amazing stuff.

When pasted together in layers, paper is almost as strong as the wood it's made from, and paper mache will last for many years if you take care of it. Your little pooch just might become a valued family heirloom or a long-treasured gift.

When I say you should 'take care of it,' I just mean you should treat it the way you would any piece of fine art.

The paper mache in this book is made out of ordinary newspaper (and a few small bits of paper towel), and a simple paste made out of flour and water. When the paper mache is dry, you'll add some color with acrylic paint, and then seal and protect your new sculpture with a good acrylic varnish.

I also give you a recipe for home-made gesso, which makes it easier to smooth out the bumps on your sculpture if you want to, or add texture for fur. It also makes a nice white ground for your paint. The gesso recipe uses drywall joint compound and PVA glue (Elmer's Glue-All). If you don't have access to these products, just skip that recipe, or use acrylic gesso from the art store. Your sculptures will still look great.

How the patterns work...

If you flip to the back of the book you'll find patterns for 27 different breeds of dogs. The patterns will help you get the proportions and outlines right, so you know your finished sculpture will look like your favorite breed, even before you start. This removes much of the guesswork (and fear) out of sculpting.

The blue lines on the patterns show you how to cut and bend the wire that will make the skeleton of your armature. Then, after filling in the forms with some foil and tape, you can position your armature by bending the wire at the joints, (shown as red dots on the patterns). The resulting sculpture will have a life-like feel, and no matter what posture you've chosen for your sculpture, all the bones and muscles will be in exactly the right place.

Does this book have everything you'll need?

No. I strongly advise you to find good photos of the breed of dog you're going to sculpt. Every professional artist uses as many references as possible, and so should you. Look for interesting poses that are characteristic of the breed, and note the color variations between individuals. Notice how some breeds are built with heavy, muscular bodies and some are thin and wiry. And also notice that within the same breed there are a lot of variations—in color patterns, ear shapes, and length of coat. The patterns can't give you that information (they're printed on flat paper, after all), but reference photos are easily available. If you have a dog in your house who is willing to pose, all the better. The more references you look

at while you sculpt, the better your final sculpture will be.

If you don't happen to have a willing canine model in the house, do a Google image search, or borrow one of the many wonderful books on dogs from the library. Children's books about dogs often have creative ideas about posing, too, and they can give you some great ideas if you'd like to add some whimsy to your sculpture.

Is this a book for kids?

This book was written with adults in mind, but a younger artist might enjoy these projects, too.

However, these projects would be discouraging for very young children. Small fingers have a hard time working with small pieces of wet, fragile paper, and it may even be difficult for them to tear the masking tape off the roll. I recommend letting younger children play around with pottery clay for now, and save this book until they're older.

A note for teachers

If you have middle school or high school students who are ready for a challenge, you might consider dedicating a few days of classroom time and have your students make their favorite dogs from this book. Be sure to make at least one yourself before the class, so you can plan the time it will take for each step. Since the sculptures use only a few layers of paper and paste, they'll dry quickly, often overnight if they're left in a warm room or in front of a fan.

Are these good toys for babies?

No! You might never ask that question, but I'll answer it anyway, just in case. Don't give your little paper mache sculpture to a baby or toddler, because the first thing they'll do is chew off the nose. Trust me, it happens. The flour and water paste won't hurt them, and a bit of newspaper probably won't hurt, either—but you don't want your baby to eat the pigments in acrylic paints or the plastic in the paint and varnish. You don't want your baby to swallow the tiny bits of foil she'll have access to after she eats the paper mache. And the wire inside is sharp.

By the way, babies aren't the only ones who eat paper mache. Puppies like it, too. Keep your sculptures up out of their reach, like you would any fine art.

One possible use for these sculptures in a nursery would be to use them in a mobile, hanging high above the baby's head. Flying dogs? Why not?

When your sculpture is finished

I would love to see how your sculptures come out. Be sure to show them off on my blog. The *Daily Sculptor's* page is a great place to leave a comment and upload a photo, because hundreds of readers subscribe to the comments on that page. There's a link to it at the top of every post.

I also hope you'll come to my blog if you have any questions about the projects in this book. I try very hard to answer every comment that comes in, usually within a few hours. Our other readers are really helpful, too, and we are always learning new things from each other.

You'll find a very positive, encouraging and nurturing community on my blog, and we would love to have you join us, at:

www.UltimatePaperMache.com

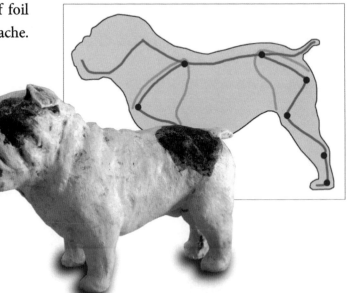

Wire Armatures

The bones of your sculpture are made with aluminum armature wire. It's easy to cut and bend.

What you'll need:

- Armature Wire—11.5 gauge (.086" or 2.15mm)
- Masking tape
- Tool for cutting and bending the wire

The Armature Wire:

Although you can use other types of wire, I recommend that you splurge for some aluminum armature wire. It isn't terribly expensive. This is the same wire that's used by artists who make figure sculptures out of clay, and it's used in the movie industry to create the inner 'bones' for stop-motion puppets. The wire is strong but fairly easy to bend, and it's easy to cut.

Armature wire is sold under two different sizing methods. Some retailers use the gauge system, and some use inches or millimeters to describe the thickness of the wire. I used 11.5 gauge wire (.086" or 2.15mm). If you make bigger sculptures, you'll want to use thicker wire.

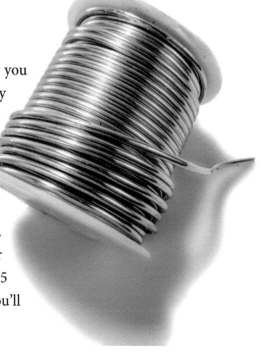

You can find armature wire online if your local art store doesn't carry it. I have purchased wire from both Amazon.com and DickBlick.com. My 50 foot roll of 11.5 gauge wire cost approximately $12, plus shipping. That much wire will make a lot of little dogs.

Can I use other kinds of wire?

You can use any wire that's easy to bend as long as it's strong enough to support the legs. If it's too hard to bend, you'll get frustrated with the project, but if it's too soft, it may not offer enough support.

Remember that uncoated steel wire will rust. If you use steel wire, it must be completely covered by masking tape to keep it dry. Otherwise, the rust will spread into the paper mache and ruin the finish on your sculpture. Don't let that stop you, though—I've made sculptures using wire I found out in the garage, and it worked just fine.

The tool:

You can bend the wire by hand, but, you'll probably need a tool to get the sharp bends that are needed for these armatures. I use needle-nose pliers, which have both cutting blades and jaws that hold and bend the wire.

The wire skeleton

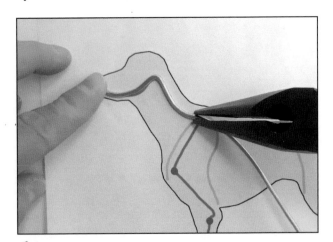

1. Lay your wire on the pattern, and bend and shape it from the nose to the tail, using the blue line on the pattern as a guide. Use your tool to cut the wire when you reach the end of the tail.

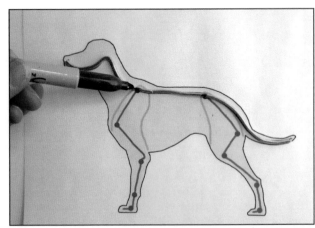

2. Use a felt tip pen or a small piece of masking tape to mark the shoulder and hip joints.

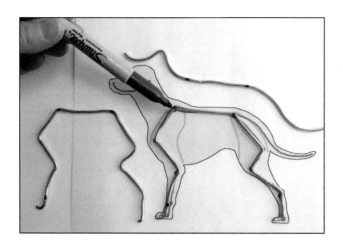

3. Bend two more pieces of wire for the legs. Each piece will go up one front leg, along the spine, and down the back leg. Take your time, and check to make sure the bends are in the right place. This takes a bit of practice. If a bend isn't in the right place, straighten the wire and bend it again—but try not to do that too often, because it could weaken the wire. Mark the shoulder and hip joints.

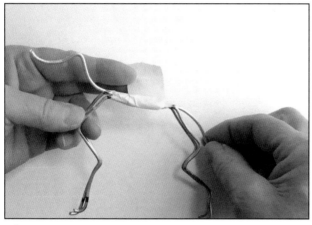

4. Line up the three wire pieces at the shoulder and hip marks, and tape them together with short pieces of masking tape.

5. Tear off a small piece of aluminum foil. This piece will be used to reinforce the shoulders.

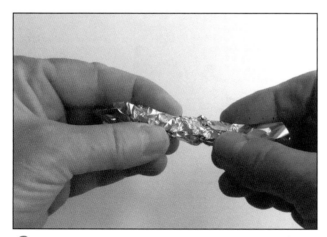

6. Crumple the piece of foil into a thin sausage shape.

7. Use your fingers to flatten the sausage into a thin strip, as shown.

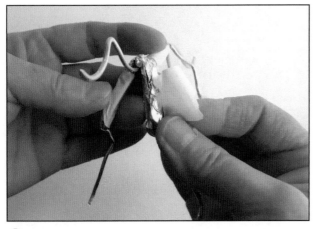

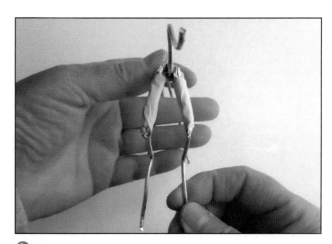

8. Fold the foil into an inverted "V" shape and place it over the shoulders. Tape the foil to the wire.

9. Bend the legs below the foil so they're straight up and down.

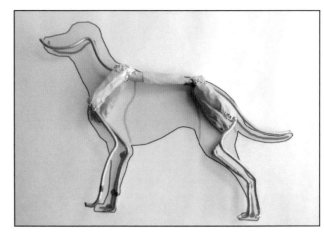

10. Reinforce the hips the same way, and bend the legs down into a natural standing position.

You should now have an armature that looks like this.

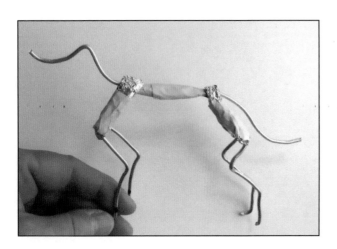

Now stand the armature on a flat surface, and make sure it's balanced. You may need to bend one of the shoulders or hips just a little so all four feet touch the table. Be sure to look at the armature from all sides, from both front and back, and from above, to make sure it looks the way you think it should. This is something you'll want to do on a regular basis as you continue building your sculpture.

Foil and Tape

You'll use small bits of foil to fill in the forms and shapes, just like you would if you were sculpting with clay.

What you'll need:

- Aluminum foil
- Masking tape
- The pattern
- Your wire armature

The aluminum foil:

Use the least expensive foil you can find at the grocery store. Cheaper foil tends to be thinner and easier to crumple into shapes. You won't need much.

The masking tape:

The masking tape will cover your armature to keep your foil in place, and it gives the paper mache something to stick to. Buy narrow tape, 1" wide or less. In many spots, you'll need to tear the masking tape lengthwise to make it even narrower. You can use the cream-colored tape or the blue kind—either one will work. Some brands stick better than others. I happen to like the Scott brand, but use whatever brand you can find. One roll is plenty.

When can I pose my Dog?

In this chapter you'll continue to follow the pattern, which shows your dog standing up on all four feet. If you want your dog to be doing something else, there are two times during this process when I recommend changing the pose:

1. When you've followed the instructions in this chapter up through Step #9. That's when you

can see the shapes of the upper body, but the legs are still free of foil and easy to bend.

2. *Or,* you can fill out the entire armature, working all the way through to the end of this chapter, and *then* do some major surgery on your pup to change his posture.

I personally prefer option #2, working through this entire chapter with my dog in a standing position. I like to see all the shapes while I'm bending the legs and neck and twisting the spine.

However, you may prefer to change the pose after Step 9, when there's less foil to cut and the wires are easier to bend. It's totally up to you.

Since you do have some options, I suggest that you read through this chapter *and* the next one, before you begin adding the crumpled foil to your armature.

Creating the outline

Work on the outlines of your dog first, using flat pieces of crumpled foil. Don't worry about filling in the roundness of the form right now. That comes later, after the outline is well-established.

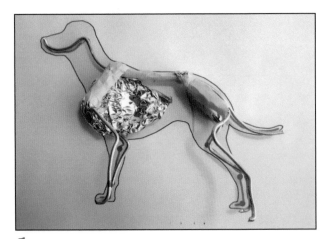

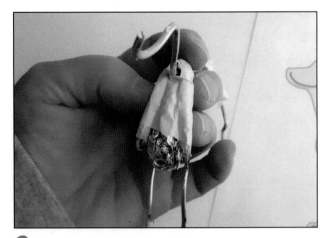

1. Crumple a ball of foil and squish it flat so it will fit between the shoulders. Place it into the chest position, and crumple the edges so they follow the outline on the pattern.

2. Tape the upper portion of the chest piece to the shoulders. Leave the leg below the shoulder free of tape.

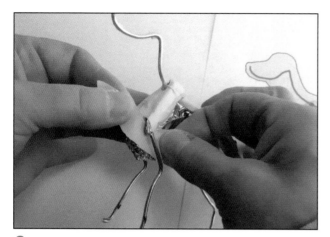

3. Cover the front of the chest with tape by putting the tape under the upper legs.

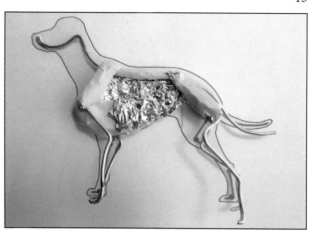

4. Add more crumpled foil to fill in the abdomen. Cover the chest and abdomen with tape.

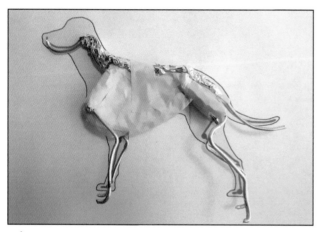

5. Add a long sausage of foil to fill in the space above the spine. Don't add foil to the tail unless it will be covered by heavy fur. Tape the foil to the armature.

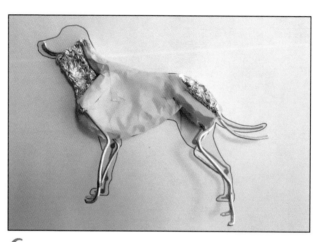

6. Add flat pieces of crumpled foil to fill in the neck and both sides of the rump. Cover with tape.

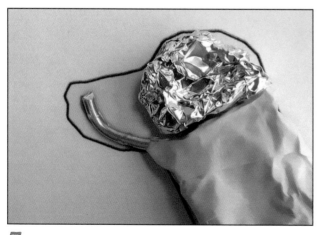

7. Put a flat ball of foil in the space for the skull.

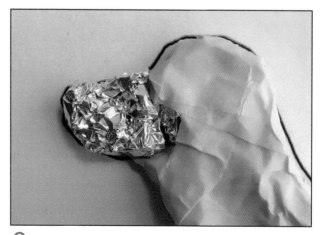

8. Then fill in the shape of the muzzle.

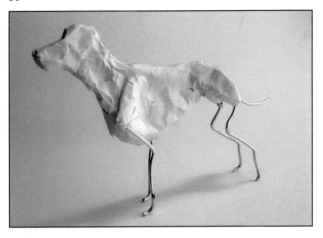

9. At this point, your armature should stand up on it's own, and it will look very flat. Stand back and look at it from a distance, and make sure the outline looks right.

You can now change the pose if you want to (see the next chapter) or wait and do it after you've followed all the following steps.

Filling in the ROUNDNESS of the FORM

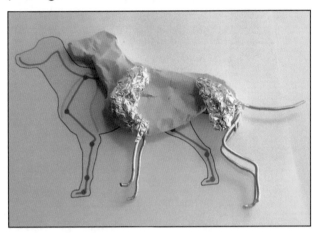

10. Fill in the shoulders and hips, using the gray lines on the pattern as a guide.

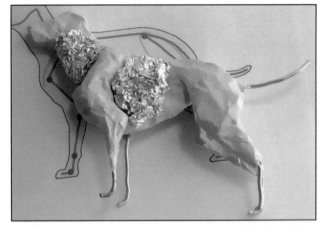

11. Pad the rib cage and neck with foil. Check your photos, since some breeds have very heavy rib cages, while some, like this Irish Setter, do not.

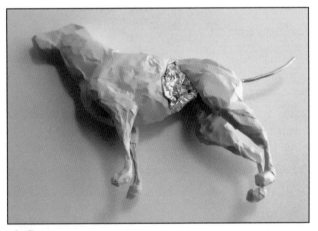

12. Add small balls of foil to the feet and pad the tummy. Cover the wire on the lower legs with tape, but don't add any foil to the lower legs unless they will be covered with heavy fur.

13. Add a flattened ball of foil to round out the cranium.

14. If needed, add foil to the lower portion of the muzzle. The muzzle is narrower along the top line and wider along the jaw, so it looks somewhat like a triangle when seen from the front.

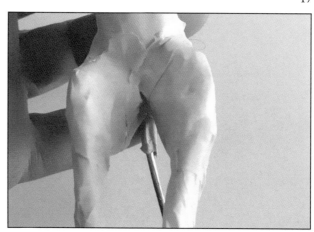

15. Add flattened pieces of foil to fill out the inner thighs. The thighs meet the lower tummy as shown above.

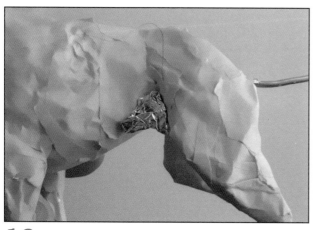

16. Add a small triangle of foil for the fold of skin that connects the upper leg to the abdomen. Cover with tape.

17. Add a little bit of foil, if needed, to round out the buttocks below the tail. The tail-end of the dog will now look like this. Cover the tail with tape.

18. Fold foil into five or six layers and cut into the shape of the ear, plus about 1/4" extra where the ear meets the head. Also leave a bit extra around the edges so you can fold it over to reinforce the ear.

Note: If the dog has long droopy ears and you will be changing the posture, you might want to put the ears on later so they don't get crumpled when you're bending the legs and neck.

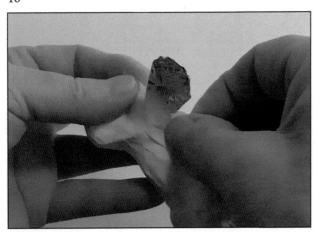

19. Fold the edges in to get the right shape and to stiffen the outer edge of the ear. Tape the ear to the head from underneath.

20. Fold the ear over the tape, and arrange it so it falls naturally. Cover the ear with tape.

Make sure the armature will still stand on a table without rocking, and step back again to look at it from a distance. The more care you put into building the armature, the more you'll like the sculpture when it's done.

Add small pieces of foil if an area doesn't seem round enough. If any sharp points of foil are sticking up where they shouldn't be, press them in with your fingers.

For Dogs with heavy coats or fluffy hairdos

Heavy fur is sculpted in the same way that the muscles are sculpted. This will include the heavy coats on dogs like the German Shepherd and the Husky, and the puffy balls of wool on a Standard Poodle' hairdo.

To fill out the bulk of fur, carefully look at your reference photos and add crumpled foil to fill out the forms, as shown in the poodle below.

1. Crumple foil into the shapes of the large masses of fur, using your reference photos as a guide.

2. Tape the foil to the dog. You can now change the pose, if you want—or leave your dog standing and move directly to the chapter on adding details.

Changing the Pose

You can now change the posture of your armature to make your dog sit, roll over, play dead, beg—whatever strikes your fancy. Or, you can leave it in the standing position, because that's good, too.

Do I have to change the pose?

No, you don't. After all, dogs *do* often stand up straight, looking attentive or regal. If you would prefer to leave your dog in a standing pose, like I did with my Irish Setter and the English Bulldog, you can skip this chapter for now.

On the other hand, changing the pose is a lot of fun.

Finding inspiration:

You'll see several common dog postures illustrated in this book, but I didn't have nearly enough room to show every breed doing all the things they're likely to do. That's why I highly recommend that you find other sources of inspiration to help you create your sculpture. You can use photos of dogs that you find in books, or do an image search on Google. You can watch videos on YouTube. Or take a video of your own dog, (which is even more fun), and stop the video at a point when the dog is doing something you think is interesting.

Another option is to simply watch your own dog carefully and notice how he positions his body when he's doing something clever or adorable. Make a few sketches, and use your sketch when you bend your armature into a new pose.

Issues to consider:

The *easiest* pose to sculpt is, of course, the standing dog, as demonstrated by the Irish Setter I made in the last chapter. She matches the pattern, so no additional changes are needed, *and* she has all four feet on the ground. That makes it easier because you don't need to make any sort of display stand or support for the sculpture, as long as you make sure the armature is well-balanced.

A dog with only three feet on the ground will also stand on it's own, as long as the legs are placed correctly (place the feet at the points of a triangle, instead of in a straight line). A dog that's lying down or sitting will also do just fine without support, and a long-tailed dog will balance well sitting up and begging.

But if the sculpted dog is standing on its hind legs, as they sometimes do when they greet their favorite person, the sculpture will need to be attached to a base so it doesn't fall over. If there are no feet *at all* on the ground, (because your champion Border Collie is flying through the air to catch a Frisbee, for instance), you'll need to think very carefully about how it will be displayed.

When should I change the pose?

As I mentioned at the beginning of the last chapter, there are two times when changing the pose is easiest:

1. Right after you complete Step #9 in the last chapter, or;
2. After all the foil has been added, and all the muscles and heavy fur have been added to the armature.

Of course, you're not limited to changing the pose just once. At almost any point in the sculpting process, you can re-bend the wires to try out a different position. As you'll see on the following pages, I made several changes in the pose of my Irish Setter, and finally decided to put her back in the standing position, because it was the best pose for showing off her elegant feathers.

Although I don't recommend doing it on purpose, you can even change the pose after the

paper mache is already dry. At that point you would need a very sharp craft knife to cut through the paper mache, but it certainly can be done—I've done it many times myself. It may seem rather drastic to cut into a sculpture that is so close to being finished, but if you aren't happy with it the way it is, change it!

What you'll need:

- Wire cutters ("diagonal pliers")
- Craft knife (optional)
- Your armature
- More foil and tape

Changing the pose, option #1

In this section, I'm working on the Irish Setter as it appeared at the end of Step #9 in the last chapter. I can only show you a few possible postures, but you can use these methods no matter which pose you choose for your own sculpture. Just remember to bend the legs only at the joints. The shoulders and hips move very little, but the spine and tail can be bent all along it's entire length, and the spine can be twisted, if needed. Be very careful to avoid cutting the wire.

1. To make the Setter sit, I bent the back legs at the knees and pulled the elbows back so the dog would sit and be well-balanced. (If I left the dog in this pose I would also bend the back feet down to a more natural position).

2. To make the head point forward instead of up at an angle, I used the pliers to cut through the foil and tape, and removed any foil that would prevent the neck from bending.

3. With a triangle of foil removed, I could then bend the head downwards.

4. The cut foil was covered with more masking tape.

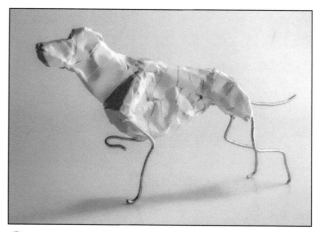

1. To make the Setter point, I straightened the hind legs, bent the front right leg at the elbow and wrist, and bent the foot on that leg so it points backwards. The foil on the neck is cut so the neck muscles can "stretch," bringing the head forward and more in line with the neck.

2. The cut foil is covered with tape, and the balance is checked. To make a dog stand up with only three feet on the ground, the feet must sit at the points of a triangle. If it keeps falling over, the feet are probably in a straight line. Keep adjusting it until it works.

Changing the pose, option #2

Although it requires more repair work, this is the option I personally prefer, especially with a complicated pose like the one below. The Shih Tzu in this demonstration will lie down with its legs stretched out behind it. It's a characteristic posture for this breed.

The Shih Tzu looked like this after following all the steps in the last chapter, except for the ears. Since she has long ears that would be crumpled while I worked on the rest of the body, I left the ears until I was happy with the pose.

1. Carefully consider the intended pose, looking at many photos that have been taken from different angles. Then cut through the foil and tape wherever the muscles need to contract or stretch. Be very careful to not snip through the wire.

2. For my Shih Tzu, a triangle of foil was removed behind the knee.

3. The back legs could then be bent backwards. The feet were bent so they're more in line with the legs.

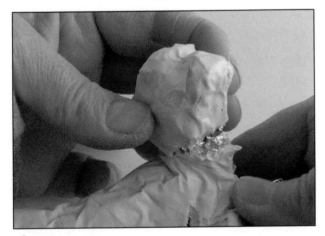

4. The foil at the front of the neck was cut and the head twisted so it's looking upwards, and slightly to the side.

5. The upper front legs were bent outwards from the shoulder, and the elbows were bent. The feet were bent forward, and the sculpture was checked to make sure it balanced properly.

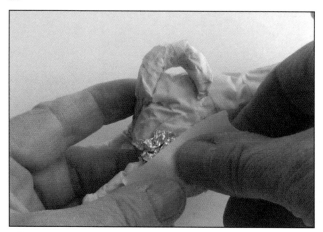

6. Foil and tape was added to repair the wounds.

7. After the repairs were made and the ears were added, the Shih Tzu now looks like this, and is ready for paper mache.

The important things to remember are:

- Muscles can stretch and contract, but bones can't. And bones can only bend, in particular ways, at the natural joints. Check your photographic resources to see where you need to bend the wires to achieve the posture you want for your sculpture.

- Any posture can be used with any dog, but some postures are more characteristic of certain breeds. For example, a Shih Tzu will often lie down in the posture shown above, but my Australian Shepherd never does that. Some American Staffordshire Terriers like to sit with their hind legs slouching sideways, and they almost never sat up straight. Bird dogs point, but English Bulldogs don't. Bulldogs *could* point if they wanted to, but they don't usually feel like it.

- Remember to bend or twist the spine if the posture calls for it. There are joints all along the spine and tail.

- Every dog has its own personality, and it shows up in the way the dog moves and how it arranges its body when resting. You can use the individuality of these postures and movements when you're sculpting a portrait of a particular dog. For instance, you might turn the generic Greyhound pattern into "Henry" the Greyhound by capturing the habitual way that Henry sprawls in his bed.

Paper and Paste

It only takes two or three layers of paper mache to cover the wire and foil armatures. It's a little messy—but that's part of the fun.

You've now been working on your little pooch for several hours, and almost all of the actual sculpting is done. Your armature probably looks a little bumpy because the crumpled foil doesn't lie down quite flat, and the little corners of your masking tape are probably sticking up here and there. But don't worry—the paper mache will cover those errant pieces of tape quite nicely, and as long as it's not *too* bumpy, the final sculpture will be smooth and pretty when it's done.

What kind of paste should I use?

The paste I recommend is made with white flour and water. It's really easy to make, it's cheap, and it works as well or better than anything else I've tried. There are a few other options, though, and I'll discuss those in a minute.

You can use almost any white flour made out of wheat for your paste: all-purpose, bleached, unbleached, or bread flour. However, *don't* use self-rising flour, which contains baking powder.

And *don't* use whole wheat flour—it might be healthier for bread, but it doesn't work for paper mache paste. It isn't sticky enough.

Can I store my paste?

You might think it will save time if you make up a big batch of paste and store what's left over for your next project. I don't recommend it. Wild yeast will try to turn your paste into sourdough starter (and alcohol), which doesn't smell very nice. Just make a small batch that you can use up in one day, and you won't have to worry about it going bad. You can always make another small batch tomorrow.

Won't it get moldy?

This is the most common question I get about paper mache from my readers, and the concern is understandable. Paper mache is made with natural materials, so it *can* be destroyed by mold if it isn't properly dried and sealed. Fortunately, you can keep your sculpture safe and beautiful for years if you make sure it dries quickly, and then seal it so it doesn't absorb moisture from the air.

Never, *ever*, paint a sculpture before it's dry all the way through. If you do, the mold spores inside the sculpture will come to life, and spots of mold will destroy the painted surface. It's best to let the sculpture dry at least an extra day after it feels completely dry on the surface, just to be safe.

The best place to dry paper mache is in front of a small fan. If you're working on your sculpture during the winter, you might be able to put it over a furnace vent. (Don't put the sculpture too close to an electric heater or a fire, because it could ignite.) Since these sculptures are very small, you can also dry them in the oven, at 200° F (93° C).

When your sculpture is dry and painted, you'll want to seal it completely with a good acrylic varnish. This will keep it from absorbing moisture from the air, and it helps protect the paint from scratches.

And remember that it isn't a good idea to display your sculpture in the bathroom near a shower, or anywhere that's usually damp. Consider this the rule of thumb: if it isn't a good place to display an original watercolor painting, it isn't a good place for paper mache, either.

But I live in the tropics...

In some areas of the world, the air is so damp that it's almost impossible to get *anything* dry before mold takes over. If you live in a very humid climate, add a few drops of household bleach or clove oil to your paste to slow down the mold. Some people add salt to their paste instead. Or use Elmer's Art Paste (available at art stores and online), because it doesn't seem to attract mold.

If your sculpture won't dry in front of a fan, dry it in an oven at 200° F (93° C). Remember to paint it and seal it just as soon as it's dry all the way through so it doesn't get damp again from moisture in the air.

Allergic to gluten?

You can use liquid laundry starch instead of the wheat paste if you or someone in your family is allergic to the gluten in wheat. You could also use the Elmer's Art Paste, which is made out of methyl cellulose.

The paper

The "skin" on your dog will be made with torn pieces of newspaper.

Dogs with long hair may also need a few sheets of two-ply kitchen paper towels for their fur. If you're making a dog with wrinkles, you can use the paper towels, or get some blue shop towels from the hardware store or the automotive department at Wal-Mart. The shop towels don't have a bumpy texture like the regular paper towels you buy for your kitchen. We'll be talking about fur and wrinkles in the Details chapter, beginning on page 36.

How to make paper mache paste

1. Put some flour in a small bowl. You won't need very much for these small sculptures—three tablespoons should be enough. If you run out, you can always make some more.

2. Add a little hot tap water, stir, check the consistency, and add more water if the paste is still too thick. The exact amount you need depends on how thick you like your paste, and how much moisture is in the flour before you start. Very warm water makes a smoother paste.

3. You can use a spoon, a fork, or an immersion blender to mix the flour and water. The blender will make the paste smooth very quickly, but you can get the same result with a spoon if you're patient.

4. When the lumps are all gone, your paste should be smooth and the consistency of heavy cream.

Tearing the paper

1. First, tear off the hard cut edge, and discard it. (Don't use the coated paper that's printed with ads—it's too hard, and it doesn't work for paper mache. Just use the regular part of the paper that the news and comics are printed on.)

2. Then tear the paper into strips. You'll need some really thin strips and some strips that are wider, perhaps 1 ½" or so. To save time and create the strongest 'skin,' use the largest piece you can in any particular spot.

Add paper mache to your Dog

1. Put plastic down on your workspace to catch the drips and make clean-up easier.

2. You can smear the paste over the dog and then lay on the strips of paper, but I personally prefer to lay the paper strip on the paste and then remove the excess on the side of the bowl, as shown.

3. Lay the wet paper over the sculpture and press it down so it lies firmly against the tape.

4. To cover the upper legs, use a thin piece of paper and roll it around the leg.

5. The paper will naturally want to lie in a certain direction, depending on the shapes beneath it. Smooth down the paper so there's no air beneath the paper mache.

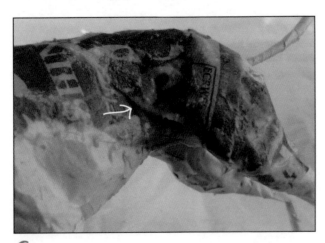

6. Check carefully to make sure no edges pop back up, like the one shown here.

Making paper mache smooth:

Paper mache always comes out a little bit uneven. It's just part of the charm of this particular material. However, there are some easy ways to have fewer bumps or hard ridges on your finished sculpture:

- Start with the smoothest possible armature by pressing down any unwanted bumps on the foil that would show up on the finished sculpture.
- Make sure the hard cut edges of the newspaper have been torn off, as shown on the previous page. Cut edges leave a sharp line on the surface of your sculpture.
- Completely saturate the paper with paste. Wet newspaper will mold into almost any shape, but dry paper won't.
- Press the paper onto the armature with your fingers. Don't allow any air bubbles to form under the paper in the dips. Pressing the paper also distributes the paste more evenly.
- Don't rush the process. Your sculpture will come out best if you take your time.

7. If an edge won't stay down, use another piece of paper to cover the upturned edge.

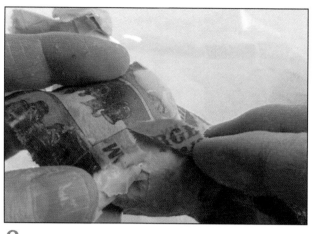

8. If the paper can't follow the contour because there's too much of a dip, tear the paper…

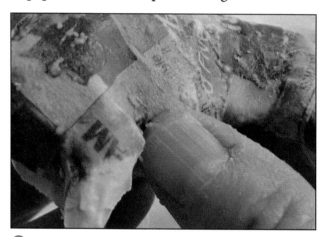

9. …and then smooth down the two sides. If a gap is left where the paper was torn, add another small piece of paper mache to cover it.

10. To cover the tail, tear a thin, long strip and lay one end on the dog's rump. This will anchor the tail's paper mache to the rest of the body.

11. Carefully wind the rest of the strip around the tail, making sure it lies flat, with no air pockets underneath. Do the lower legs the same way.

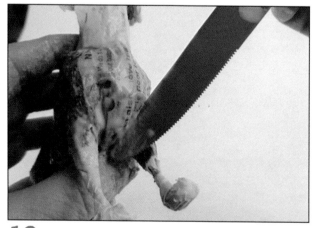

12. In areas that need to have a sharp crease, like the valley between the front legs and the chest, press the dull side of a knife into the paper mache, as shown.

13. The feet are tiny, so they're hard to cover smoothly. Wrap the lower leg and foot the same way as the tail in steps 10 and 11. Then tear a very small piece of paper to lay over the end of the foot.

14. Smooth this piece over the foot, and carefully press down all the way around, so all the paper mache lies tight over the masking tape.

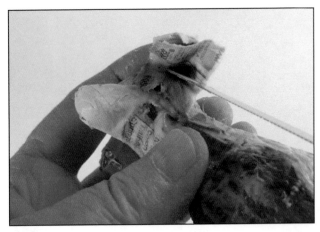

15. Lay paper mache on the neck and over the forehead, under the ear.

16. Unfold the ear just enough so you can put a piece of paper underneath, with the end on the cheek. Use a knife to push the paper deep into the underside of the ear.

17. Press the paper mache against the ear on the inner side, and then wrap the edges around to the front.

Note: If you aren't happy with the shape of the ears after the paper mache is dry, you can use a pair of heavy-duty scissors to cut them into a better shape. The cut edge can be smoothed over with a small piece of paper towel dipped in paste.

18. Put another piece of paper over the top of the dog's head and extending down over the ear. Fold the edges to the underside of the ear.

19. Now gently bend the ear into it's final shape. The foil underneath will hold it into shape until the paper mache dries.

20. Put a piece of paper over the muzzle, and tear the end so it can fold over the nose.

21. Smooth the paper mache over the muzzle, making sure that it lies tight against the masking tape, with no air gaps underneath.

22. When the entire dog has been covered with one layer of paper mache, go back and give it another coat over the body and upper legs. You don't need to wait until the first layer dries. You may not want to add more paper mache to the lower legs, tail, ears or muzzle if you're making a smooth-coated dog. More layers of paper mache could make these areas too heavy.

Checking the shapes

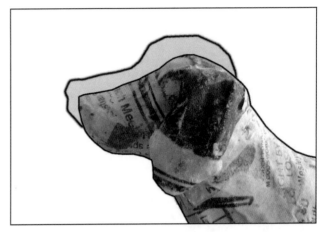

Let your dog dry overnight, or at least until it's easy to handle without damaging the wet paper mache. Then check to make sure everything looks the way you want it to. If any strips of paper have come loose, cover the loose edges with another strip oaf paper and paste. Check the outline, too.

For instance… My Irish Setter isn't *exactly* like the pattern, but I'm happy with her—except for the head. When I compare the top line of the head to the pattern, I see that the outline isn't right. This needs to be fixed before the sculpture is painted.

For this particular problem, I tear a small rectangle of paper, add paste to one side, and fold it several times.

Then I paste the folded rectangle onto the head to create a sharper angle between the muzzle and the forehead. This angle is called a 'stop' on a dog.

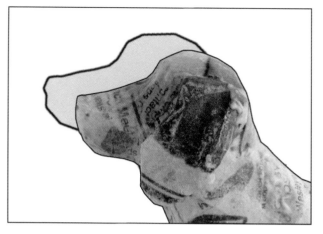

Two more rectangles of paper cover the folded piece, to smooth over the transitions.

Now when I place the sculpture over the pattern, the outline looks much better. Almost any problem area can be easily fixed in a similar way.

The paper mache is almost Done ...

In the next chapter we'll add fur, wrinkles, open mouths, noses, and other details.

Adding Details

You can now add a few pieces of paper-towel mache to add details and textures to your sculpture.

You can use some of the ideas in this chapter if you want, or leave them off—it depends entirely on the style you're trying to achieve.

Note: If you use two-ply paper towels, pull the two plies apart and use just one ply, or paste the two plies back together before adding them to your sculpture.

Nose

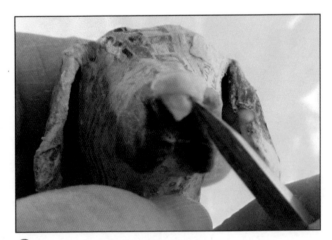

1. Tear a tiny piece of paper towel for the nose. Dip the paper in the paste, then roll or fold the paper towel piece into an itty-bitty triangle. If you want a more whimsical look, you can roll the nose into a ball.

2. Put a dab of paste on the muzzle, and attach the triangle, point down. You can use the tip of your scissors to make an indentation for the nostrils, if you want.

Happy Mouth

1. Roll up a very small sausage of crumpled foil, shape it into a "U," and tape the ends below the muzzle as shown. The lower jaw is shorter than the upper jaw, and narrower.

2. Use more masking tape or small strips of paper mache to cover the foil mouth. Use a tool to push the tape together in the center of the "U" shape, so there's a dip where the tongue will go.

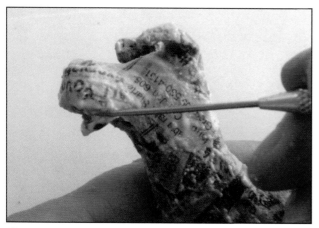

3. Use small strips of paper when covering the mouth with paper mache. Use a sharp tool to push the sides of the mouth into a smile, if desired.

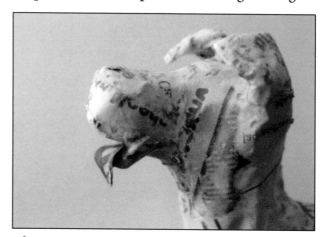

4. You can also add a tongue, made with three layers of newspaper pasted together and cut to shape.

Teeth

If the tongue lolls to the side, you may want to add tiny teeth. For this example I used mustard seeds glued on with white glue (Elmer's Glue-All, or PVA glue), with a small piece of paper towel pasted in front of them to form a lower lip. It gave my Golden Retriever a goofy smile.

If the upper teeth show, as in a snarl, you can use rice or other sharp seeds for the canines.

Eyebrows ∿

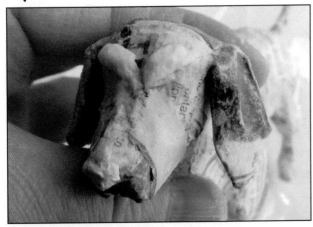

1. Roll up two small pieces of pasted paper towel into tiny sausages, and place on the head for the eyebrow bone.

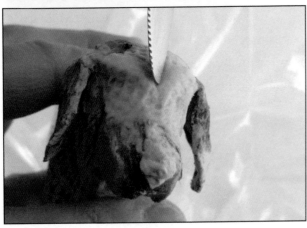

2. Add another piece of one-ply paper towel over the eyebrows to give them a smooth transition with the rest of the head.

Press down on the paper towel to smooth out the bumps (they won't smooth entirely, but we'll take care of that later). Then use the dull side of a table knife or your finger to make a nice dent between the eyebrows, as shown.

If you don't like working with the texture of the paper towels, use the blue shop towels from the hardware store instead.

Feathers and long fur ∿

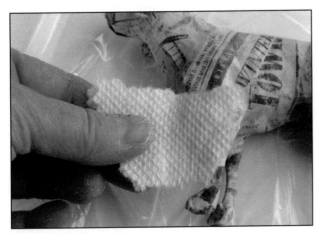

1. Tear a piece of paper towel in the shape shown above. It should be as high as the space between the elbow and the wrist.

2. If it's two-ply paper, pull the plies apart. Add paste to one piece.

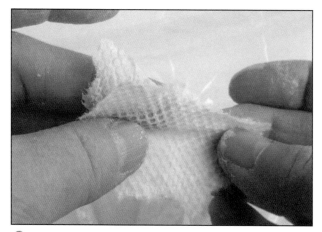

3. Then paste the two plies back together. You'll be tempted to skip this step, but it keeps the two plies from coming apart.

4. Add more paste to the back of your piece, and fold it around a front leg, as shown. Press down on the paper towel that's around the leg to flatten the bumpy pattern a little.

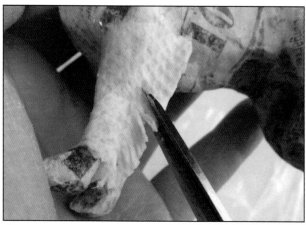

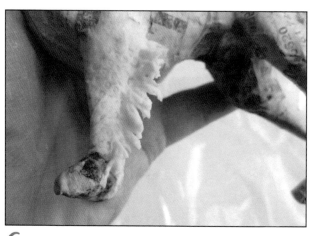

5. Trim the piece, using your chosen photographic model as a guide. Different dogs of the same breed will have more or less feathering on their legs and tail. Use sharp scissors to cut the paper into a fringe.

6. Ruffle the hairs apart to make them seem more natural, but try not to touch the fringe too much after it's cut, or all the individual hairs will try to stick back together. Do the tail the same way.

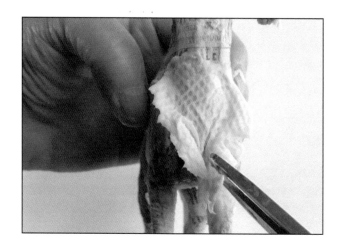

7. To add longer fringe to the chest, paste a triangular piece of towel to the chest and scrunch the bottom of the triangle together, as shown. Cut the fringe. Press the paper over the chest with your fingers to flatten the paper towel.

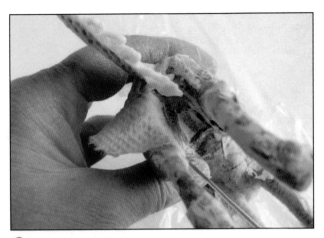

8. Paste two plies of paper towel together and paste one edge to the inside of the buttocks below the tail, as shown.

9. Then add another piece on outside of the buttocks, pressing the two pieces together behind the leg. Trim to shape with sharp scissors.

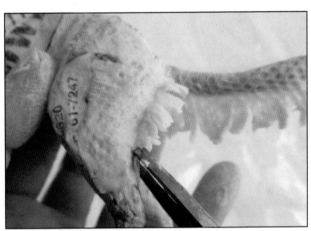

10. Cut the pasted paper into a fringe.

11. Paste together three plies of paper towel, and paste this combined piece to the chest and tummy as shown. Cut the overhanging paper into a fringe.

12. Use two plies of pasted-together paper towel for the ears. Fold the towel around the edges of the ear, and cut the bottom fringe. Press on the paper towel to flatten it against the ear.

Heavy Wrinkles

Many smooth-coated dogs, like English Bulldogs, Basset Hounds, and Pugs, have more skin than they really seem to need, and it falls into wrinkles. Adding wrinkles to a small sculpture is fun, and adds a lot of character to the piece.

In the examples below, I'm using paper towels with an embossed texture, because these towels are available almost everywhere. The texture can be covered with several layers of home-made gesso, but you may find it easier to use the blue shop towels that you can find at automotive supply stores and hardware stores. You can also find them in the hardware section of Walmart. The blue shop towels aren't textured, so they require less work before painting.

1. Use one ply of paper towel. Apply paste to both sides and roll it into a sausage. Lay the rolled towel where the skin folds, using photo references as a guide.

2. Continue adding more rolls of towel to fill out the wrinkles. On the Bulldog (and the Basset Hound on the next page) I also used rolled paper towels for the lips.

3. Use one ply of paper towel to cover the wrinkles. Use a knife or other tool to push the towel between the wrinkles to help define the shapes.

4. When finished, allow the damp paper towels to dry before painting.

Lighter Wrinkles

Some dogs have wrinkled skin that isn't as deeply defined as the face wrinkles on a Bulldog. The "baggy socks" on the Basset Hound's legs are an example. These wrinkles can be effectively created using just one piece of paper towel scrunched into pleats, as shown below.

1. Put paste on both sides of one ply of paper towel that has been torn long enough so it will cover the intended area after it's been scrunched. Place the towel over the area that needs wrinkles.

2. Use your fingers or a tool to push the towel into pleats. Allow to dry before painting.

Heavily textured fur

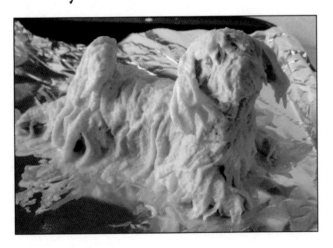

You can use the scrunched paper towel technique shown above, combined with the cut fringe that was described beginning on page 39, to create heavily textured fur. In the example shown here, the long fur fans out on the floor when the Shih Tzu is lying down. A sheet of aluminum foil was placed on a cookie sheet to keep the paper towel mache from sticking to the table, and it also allowed me to easily move the wet piece to the oven to dry.

Before You Paint

Your dog is almost done. You can now leave the paper mache just as it is, or make the paper mache smoother, or add interesting textures. The decision is up to you.

You probably see some bumps, dips or ridges in the surface of the paper mache when your sculpture is dry. This is one of the characteristics of this sculptural medium. You can now choose to leave the irregularities and go straight to painting, or take a bit of time to make it smoother, depending on your artistic style.

Many artists like to emphasize the whimsical "paper mache-ness" of their work, leaving no room for doubt about how their sculpture was made. In fact, some artists even leave the newsprint showing, and simply add a protective coat of acrylic varnish.

If you prefer to paint your little dog, you can use sandpaper or an emery board to remove any unwanted bumps or ridges in the paper mache, and then add a coat or two of the following home-made gesso recipe to get the surface of the paper mache even smoother. You can also use the gesso to create a light texture to indicate fur.

Gesso can also be used as a primer to create a nice white surface for your paint. If you don't have access to the ingredients in this recipe, you can use acrylic gesso from your local art store, instead.

What you'll need:

- Sharp box cutter or craft knife
- Fine sandpaper or emery board
- Damp sponge
- Joint compound
- White glue
- Dab of white acrylic paint (optional)

What is joint compound?

Joint compound is a product used in the building and remodeling trades. It helps builders cover the seam between two pieces of drywall (also called plaster board or gypsum board) when they're finishing new walls. You can find joint compound in the painting supplies section of Walmart and at all hardware stores and building supply stores.

If you don't happen to live in the United States, this product may be sold under a different name. For instance, according to some of my blog readers, it's called "drywall filler" in Canada and "joint filler" in the UK. To find out what it's called in other countries, go to my blog at:

http://www.ultimatepapermache.com
and type "what is joint compound called" in the search bar. Or just ask the friendly clerk at your local hardware store.

The kind of joint compound you want for the gesso recipe is the pre-mixed kind that comes in a plastic tub. You won't need very much. The last time I looked, you could get 1 quart of Sheetrock™ brand joint compound at Home Depot for less than $4. This would be enough to cover many small sculptures. If you can't find the smallest size, get the gallon size, and throw a dog sculpting party!

If you can't easily find joint compound where you live, just skip this recipe and use commercial gesso from the art supply store, or just apply a coat of white paint, instead. Using the home-made gesso is not required—it just makes it a bit easier to get a smooth or textured finish on your dog.

The glue

In the United States, the glue you'll want to buy is Elmer's Glue All™, which is available almost anywhere. If you live somewhere else, just ask for "PVA glue." Buy a small container, because you won't need very much.

The knife, sponge, sandpaper and emery board

You can often remove unwanted small bumps or ridges from paper mache with a sharp knife, but you need to be really careful to not cut too deep and leave a gap where the foil or masking tape shows. These "wounds" can be repaired with a small piece of paper and paste.

When the bump is in a spot that's too hard to reach, or if it's just a small amount of texture that you want to smooth out in the final coat of gesso, I like to use an emery board. Of course you can use a small piece of fine sandpaper instead. You may need to tear the sandpaper into a narrow strip in order to reach in under the legs.

For smoothing the dried home-made gesso, a damp sponge is the perfect tool. It will smooth out the surface of the gesso without putting any dust into the air. Remember, if you do use sandpaper, be sure to use a mask so you don't get dust in your lungs.

I like to put off any sanding until after one thin coat of gesso has been applied to my sculptures. It covers the busy printing on the newspaper strips, so it's much easier to see the surface of the paper mache. Also, the gesso will cover many small irregularities, which saves me the trouble of sanding.

How to make the home-made gesso:

I can't give you a specific recipe for the gesso because different brands of joint compound contain different amounts of water. Fortunately, a recipe isn't really needed, anyway. Put a dab of joint compound in a bowl, add white glue and just a small dab of white paint to make the gesso more opaque. Mix the ingredients until smooth.

Self-leveling gesso:

For a mixture that will leave few brush marks, mix until it looks like heavy cream when it drips off the spoon. If brush marks remain visible, add a little more glue, and mix again. This works well when you don't want any texture at all.

For heavy texture:

Use more joint compound in the mix so it will hold soft peaks, like whipped cream. You can use this thicker mixture to smooth out irregularities in the paper mache and to cover the embossed texture of paper towels. It's also great for adding texture for fur. Don't put it on too thickly in one coat, though, or it may crack when it dries.

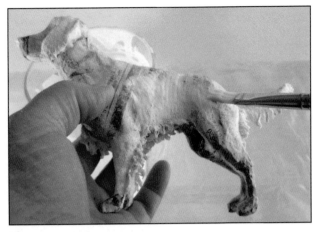

1. Brush the gesso over the paper mache. The first coat will dry quickly, and will cover most of the designs and printing on the newspaper.

2. When the first coat of gesso is dry, look over the sculpture to find any spots that need to be smoother. Don't worry about the texture of the paper towel, because the next coat or two of gesso should cover it.

3. Use your sharp knife to remove any ridges, like the one shown above. Be careful so you don't cut all the way through the paper mache and expose the foil underneath.

4. Problem areas between the legs are easier to reach with your emery board or a small strip of fine sandpaper.

5. When the bumps have been removed, give your dog a second coat of gesso. Use your damp sponge or fine sandpaper to smooth the dried gesso, if needed. If you're making a smooth-coated dog and you like the way it looks, you can paint the dog as soon as the gesso is dry. Or you can add additional texture, as shown on the next page.

For a very smooth coat...

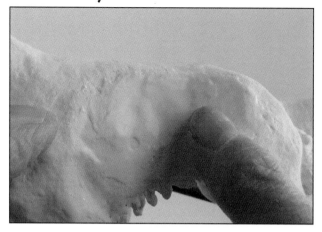

Brush the last layer of gesso onto a small area of the dog. Then dip a finger into water and glide your damp finger over the gesso, smoothing it out.

For a wavy coat...

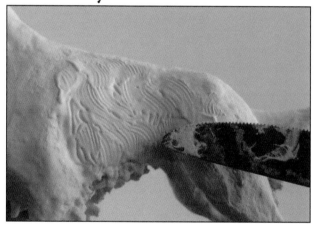

Create parallel lines in a wave pattern with a serrated knife.

Texture over texture...

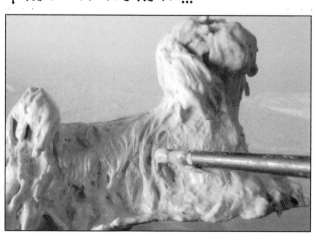

For long hair....

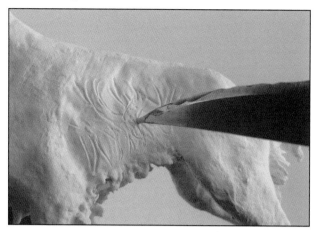

Use the sharp point of a knife or the handle of your paintbrush to draw lines in the gesso. Be sure to follow the natural growth of the fur.

To soften the texture...

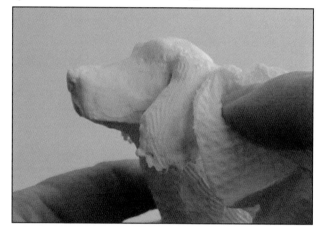

When the gesso is dry, dampen a paper towel or sponge with water and gently rub the gesso until you have the texture you want.

If you created a heavy texture using the paper towel method in the previous chapter, you can add even more detail by brushing on the gesso and then using the tip of a knife or the handle of a brush to create lines to indicate finer hairs.

When you're happy with the surface, either smooth or textured, allow the gesso to dry completely. You're then ready to paint.

Painting and Finishing

There's an almost unlimited number of ways that you can paint your little dogs, depending on your own artistic style.

In fact, if you'd like to leave the newsprint showing and not paint your sculpture at all, that's fine, too. To see some amazing examples of the many creative ways people have found to paint (and not paint) paper mache dogs, go to Pinterest.com and do a search for "paper mache dogs." If you do decide to let the newsprint show, you still need to seal the paper with an acrylic varnish to protect it from dirt and moisture in the air

Since there are hundreds of different ways that you could paint your dog, you should consider the following as just a starting place. After you've made a few of these little sculptures, you're sure to develop a style of your own.

What you'll need:

- Acrylic paint or craft paint
- Golden Acrylic Glazing Liquid (optional)
- Matte acrylic varnish
- Small brushes

Colors:

You can paint almost any dog in their natural colors with the following paints:

- Yellow Ochre
- Raw Sienna
- Burnt Sienna
- Burnt Umber
- Cadmium Red Light
- Titanium White
- Black.

These are the colors I used for the dogs I made to illustrate this book. I like the Liquitex Soft Body paints, but any acrylic paint or craft paint will work just fine.

The acrylic glazing liquid is used to make the fur texture stand out, as you'll see in the next few pages. I also like using it to give a sculpture an antique or folk-art feel. You don't need to use it if you don't want to. There are other brands of glazing liquid, but they all work a bit differently. The Golden brand is the one I prefer.

Painting a white Dog

1. Give your dog a base coat using Titanium White and a small dab of Yellow Ocher. (Any of the earth colors will add a warm tone to the white, and make it more interesting.)

2. You can add light fur marks with the brush strokes, as shown in Step 1, or add a wooly texture by dabbing the end of the brush, as shown above. Allow the paint to dry.

3. Paint the eyes and nose with the black paint.

4. When the black is dry, mix a small amount of Burnt Umber with a larger amount of Golden Acrylic Glazing Liquid.

5. Make sure you have a damp paper towel handy. Then brush the dark glaze over a section of the sculpture.

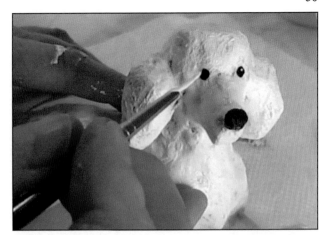

6. Immediately wipe off the glaze, using the damp paper towel. Leave just enough to show the texture of the fur, without making the white coat look dirty.

7. Allow the glaze to dry completely, preferably overnight. Then add a tiny speck of white for a reflection in the eye. You can use a very small paint brush for this, or the sharp point of a needle that has been dipped in the white paint.

8. Give your sculpture a coat or two of matte acrylic varnish, and allow to dry. Your sculpture is now officially done. (If you want to sign it, you can use a small paint brush or a fine permanent marker).

Some dogs are mostly white, like some Skye Terriers, but have darker ears or spots.

Painting a solid color other than white

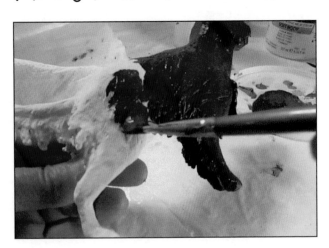

Some dogs, like the Irish Setter and the Golden Retriever, have coats that appear to be all one color. However, when you look closely you see a lot of variation in their coats.

I painted this Irish Setter with a mixture of Burnt Sienna, Raw Sienna, and Burnt Umber. Try to vary the color as you paint to keep the coat interesting. For the setter I used paint with more Burnt Umber on the feathers, and used the redder mixture on the back.

The Golden Retriever was painted with a mixture of Raw Sienna, Titanium White, and a dab of Burnt Sienna. The feathers on the arms and the ears are lighter than the body.

The tongue was painted with a mixture of Cadmium Red Light, Titanium White, and a small dab of Yellow Ochre. The lower lip, eyes and nose are black (see finished dog below).

A glaze could have been used on both of these bird dogs, but I decided not to. If you want to make the texture of the fur stand out more, or if you think it would make the coat more interesting, follow the steps as shown for the Standard Poodle, beginning with Step 4.

Almost all solid-colored dogs can be painted with a mixture of the colors listed on page 48.

Short-haired Dogs with solid spots

The edges of a spot can be blended into the body color (or the color of another spot) with a dry brush or by smudging with your finger or a damp paper towel. Or you can leave the edges sharp, like they are on the Basset Hound shown here. Check your reference photos to know which technique will work best for your particular dog.

Some dogs, such as Pugs and Doberman Pinschers, are all one color on the body and anther color on the face or legs. These colored areas usually blend in with the body color where the edges meet.

Short-haired Dogs with Brindle spots

1. Paint a heavy coat of the lightest color over the spot. For this red I used Raw Sienna, Burnt Sienna and Yellow Ochre.

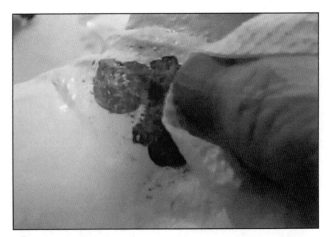

2. Immediately pounce a dry paper towel over the spot. This will give a mottled area. Allow the spots to dry. (The white area of the body will need to be cleaned up later with more white).

3. When the first color is dry, paint over it with a heavy coat of black or Burnt Umber.

4. Immediately pounce a dry paper towel over the darker color, leaving another patch of mottled color.

5. When the dark color is dry, clean up the white areas with more white paint, and allow that to dry. The finished spots will look like the ones on this English Bulldog. Many different breeds of dogs have brindled patches, including Great Danes, American Staffordshire Terriers, Boxers and Greyhounds.

Colored Spots on a Long-Haired Dog

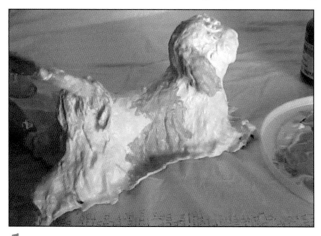

1. Paint the lightest colors first, and allow the paint to dry.

2. Then paint the darker colors, blending in as needed.

3. Mix acrylic glazing liquid with Burnt Umber, and paint over a section of the dog.

4. Immediately wipe off the excess glaze with a damp paper towel, leaving the dark color in the deeper recesses of the textured coat.

The glaze in the shadows will bring out the heavy texture, and helps to bring the colors together.

Salt and Pepper Coat, Dapple and Blue Merle

You can use the acrylic glazing liquid mixed with black to create a coat of mixed black and white hairs. Use very little pigment and lots of glaze, and don't mix it very much on the palette. The brush will leave streaks of darker color alternating with streaks of transparent color, as shown on the back of this Dandy Dinmont Terrier.

This technique would work well with the grey fur of some Huskies, and on a Welsh Corgi or Border Collie that has a Blue Merle coat. It would also work for a Dachshund with a dappled coat.

Adding a bit of pink

For the Basset Hound's tummy I used Cadmium Red Light, Titanium White and a dab of Yellow Ocher. To blend the pink into the white tummy, I used a paper towel as shown for the Bulldog's brindle spots.

The same color works well for tongues, and for the white area that shows below droopy eyes, as shown above .

When the paint is DRy:

Be sure to add a coat or two of acrylic varnish, to protect the paint and seal the sculpture.

Patterns

Now that you've read the preceding chapters, you're ready to choose a pattern and start sculpting!

Remember:

Use these patterns along with good photographs that show you the colors, ear shapes and various coats and colors for the breed you've chosen. You'll also want photos showing dogs doing as many things as possible, and taken from many different angles. Good photos will help you choose the exact pose you want for your sculpture. The more references you have on hand, the more you'll like your finished sculpture.

What about mixed-breed dogs?

If you're making a portrait of a mixed breed dog, you probably won't find a pattern in this book that perfectly matches your dog. However, you can still use the patterns by mixing and matching pieces of different patterns.

For instance, I have a mixed-breed dog that's half Lhasa Apso and half Cavalier King Charles Spaniel. I could use the Cavalier pattern on page 58 for his head and body, and use the Shih Tzu pattern on page 57 for the shorter legs and curled-up tail. It would be easy to combine the two with a pencil and a piece of tracing paper.

You can do the same thing if you want to make a purebred dog that isn't included in the book. Look closely at the body shapes of your chosen breed, and then find patterns that will help you achieve those shapes in your sculpture. For instance, there's no Labrador Retriever in the book, but you might be able to combine the body and head of the Golden Retriever with the longer legs of the Irish Setter, paint him black, and there's your Lab.

Do I have to follow the patterns exactly?

No, you sure don't. Like a bit of whimsy? Go ahead and play. Have a dog that doesn't quite fit the breed's pattern because he's a little taller or heavier than my drawing? Change the pattern to fit the dog—and remember to have fun!

Lap Dogs

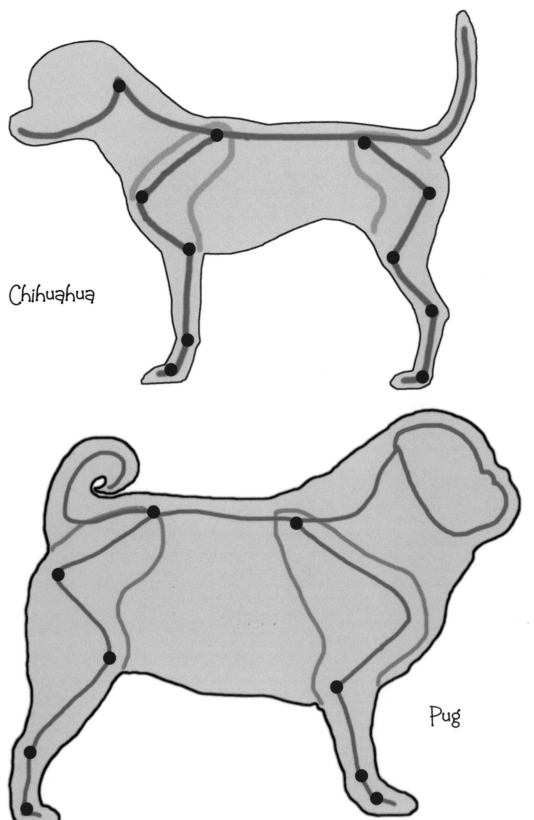

Chihuahua

Pug

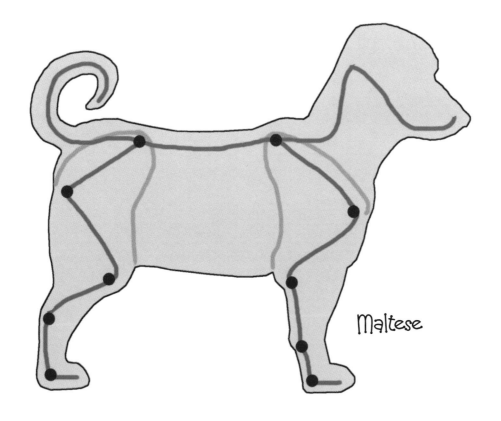

Maltese

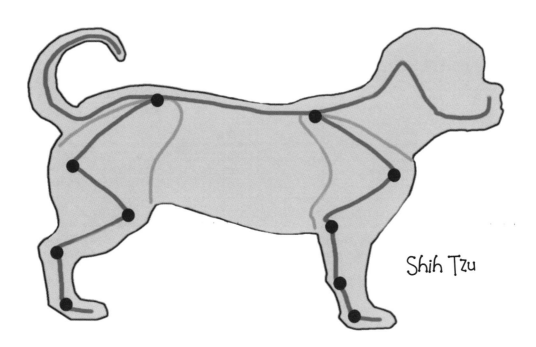

Shih Tzu

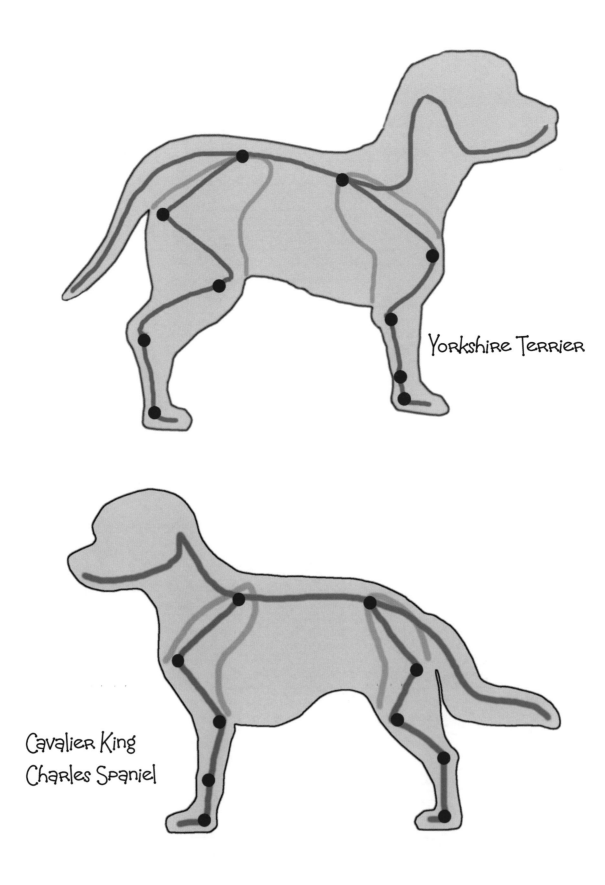

Yorkshire Terrier

Cavalier King
Charles Spaniel

Terriers

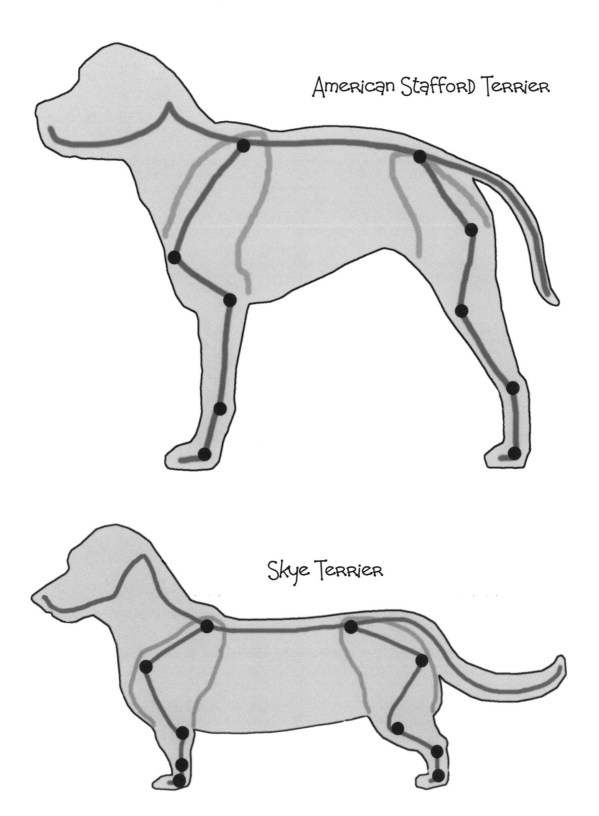

American Stafford Terrier

Skye Terrier

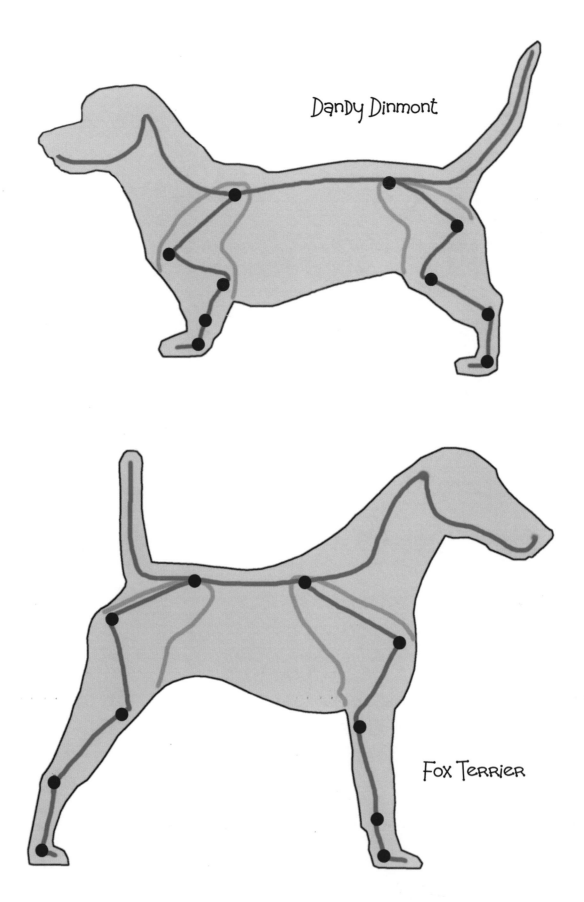

Dandy Dinmont

Fox Terrier

Bird Dogs

Golden Retriever

Irish Setter

Standard Poodle

Herding Dogs

Welsh Corgi

Border Collie

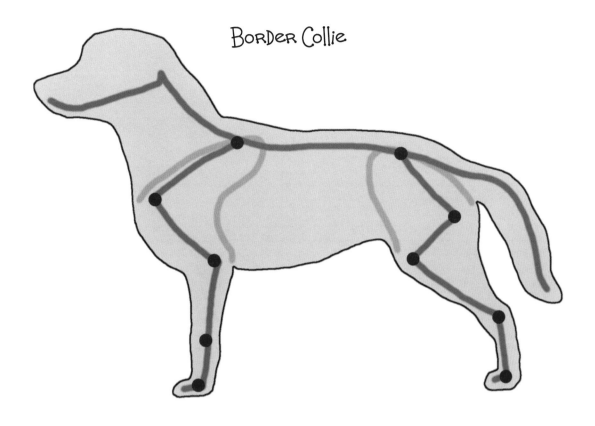

German Shepherd

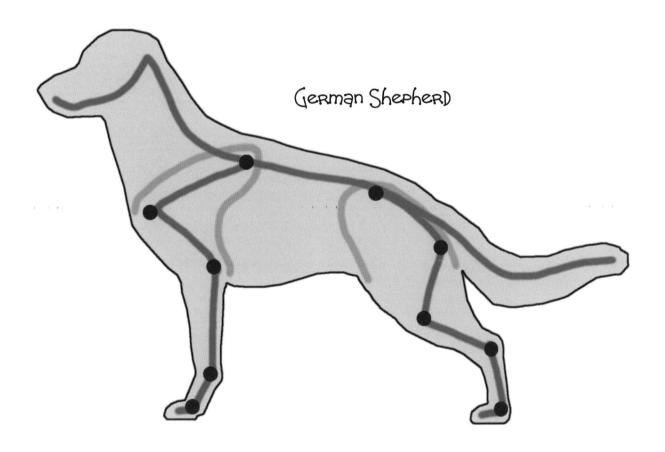

Hounds

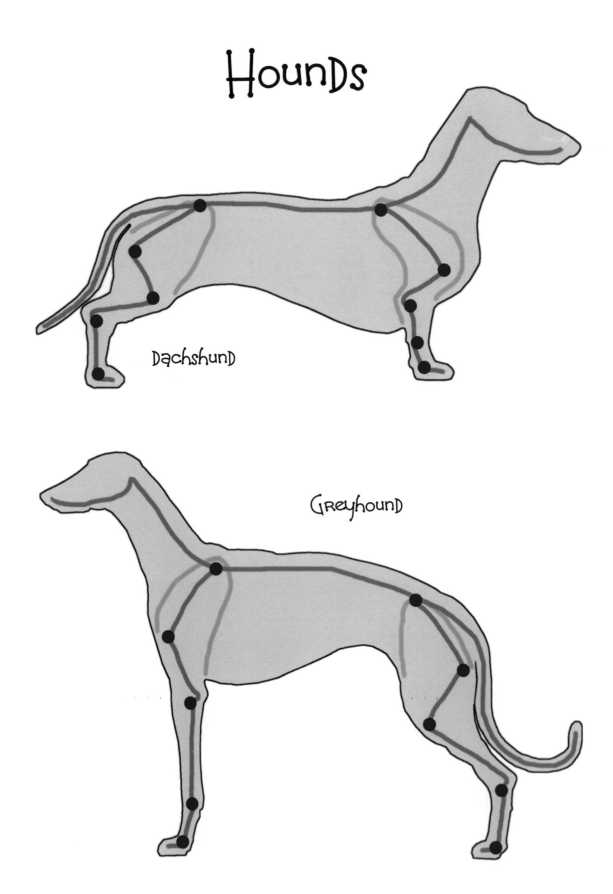

Dachshund

Greyhound

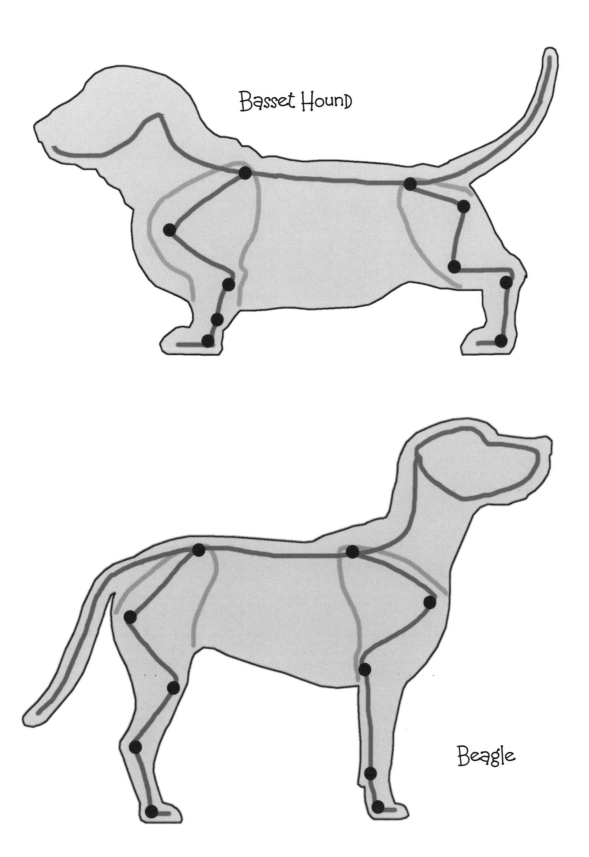

Basset Hound

Beagle

Working Dogs

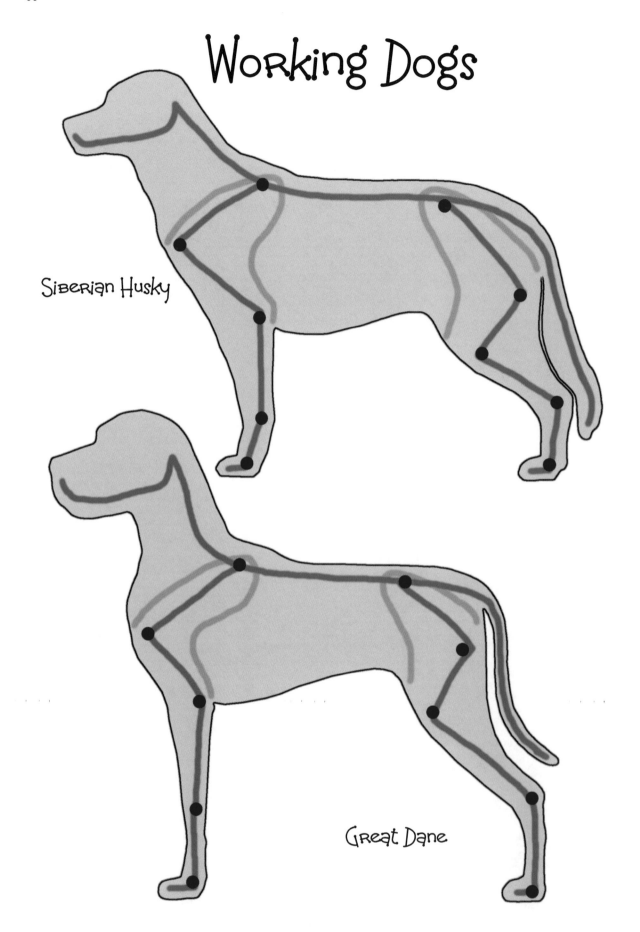

Siberian Husky

Great Dane

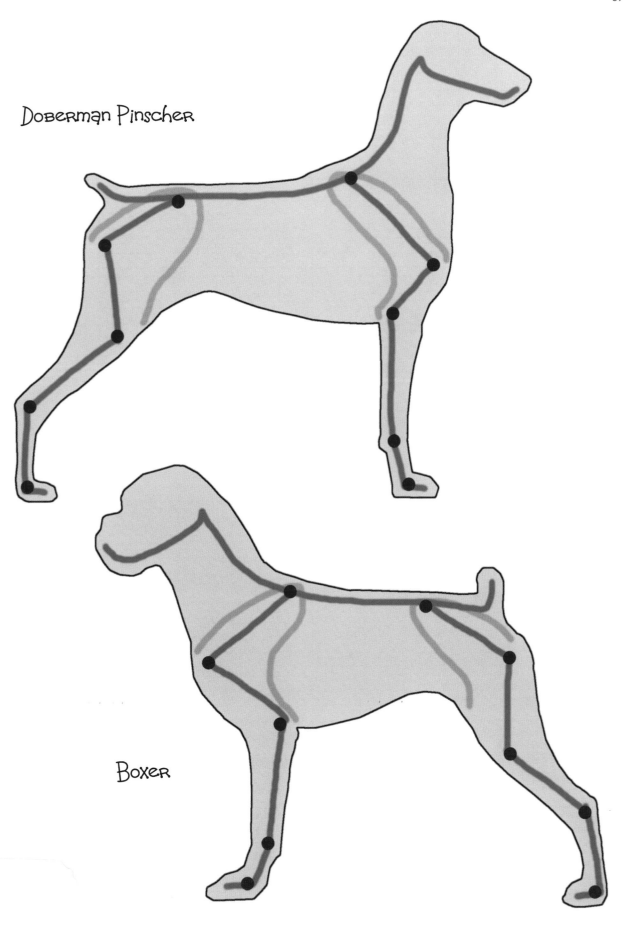

Doberman Pinscher

Boxer

Non-Sporting Dogs

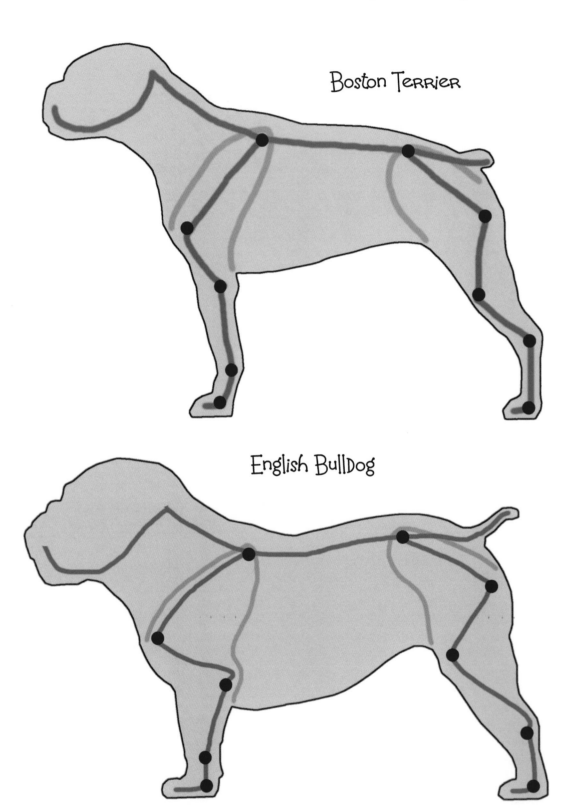

Boston Terrier

English Bulldog

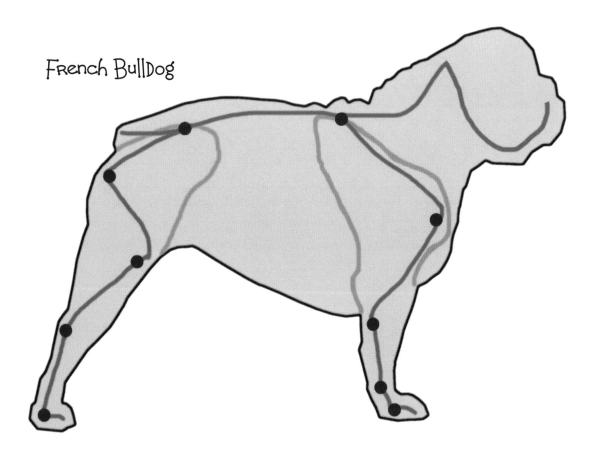

French BullDog

About the author:

I love animals, especially dogs, and my home is full of paper mache sculptures and masks. I also love to experiment and try new things. My Paper Mache Clay recipe, and, more recently, my Silky-Smooth Air-Dry Clay recipe, have been adopted enthusiastically by sculptors and doll-makers from around the world—and my "shop-towel and fast-setting paper mache paste" method has been a huge hit with new mask makers. I now write and sculpt full-time, and I'm always looking for ways to make sculpting easier, less expensive, and more fun for artists everywhere!

Also by Jonni Good:

- *Make Animal Sculptures with Paper Mache Clay*
- *How to Make Masks!*
- *How to Make Adorable Baby Animal Dolls*
- *Endangered Animals Color and Learn Book*

You can find all of my books on your favorite online book store.

Visit me online!

Over 4,000 people visit my blog every day to read the tutorials, watch the videos, post photos of their own work, and join the lively conversation with other artists. I hope you'll drop by soon. And be sure to subscribe to my newsletter, so you never miss a tutorial or post.

www.UltimatePaperMache.com

Made in the USA
Lexington, KY
09 July 2014